Grammar Made Easy

for Infants

Books 3 and 4

By

C .M. Greenidge

First edition 2022

Books 3 and 4 Combined and Revised

Cover design by Cheryl Greenidge
Edited by E. Jerome Davis
Published by Cheryl .M. Greenidge

ISBN: 9798846406230

ABOUT THE AUTHOR

Cheryl Greenidge attended St. Martin's Girl's School, the Princess Margaret Secondary School and the Barbados Community College. In 1988, she started her career as a primary school teacher. In 1997, she enrolled at the Erdiston Teacher's Training College where she completed her Diploma in Education. In 2005, Cheryl was made Early Childhood Coordinator at the St. Martin's - Mangrove Primary School. Cheryl's years of experience in the infants' department have greatly assisted her in compiling the material for this book. She is the author of 'Word Building for Infants', 'A Spelling and Reading Aid for Beginners', 'Grammar Made Easy for Infants' – Books 1, 2, 3 and 4, 'First Steps to Mathematics', 'Second Steps to Mathematics' and 'Third Steps to Mathematics'.

CONTENTS

PREFACE

"Grammar Made Easy for Infants Books 3 and 4 Combined" is a follow up to "Grammar Made Easy for Infants - Books 1 and 2 Combined". It covers all the concepts in Books 1 and 2 combined, but **at a higher level**.

Every effort has been made to include age-appropriate vocabulary and to present the concepts in a simple but interesting manner. The many activities are presented in a variety of ways in order to reinforce the concepts. A feature of the text is the inclusion of Barbadian references which help to create that connection between child and activity and generate discussion.

"Grammar Made Easy for Infants - Books 3 and 4 Combined" although specially designed for the 6 – 8 age group, may be helpful to older children who have not mastered the concepts presented

Section 1

Vowels

A and An

✿ Circle only the vowels and then sort all the letters in the correct boxes.

n	a	r	t	e	m	u	f
p	l	i	d	o	s	b	

vowels

_ _ _ _ _

consonants

_ _ _ _

_ _ _ _

✿ Write the missing vowels for the words.

dr_m   b_d   f_sh   _r_ng_

✿ Write the missing consonants for the words.

__ __ee   _o_k   s_ oo_   _a_ p

✿ Circle only the words which begin with a vowel and then sort all the words in the correct boxes.

okra, cake, icicle, bucket, apron, goat, elbow, pole

Words Beginning with Vowels

_____

_____

_____

_____

Words Beginning with Consonants

_____

_____

_____

_____

✿ We write 'an' before most words which begin with a vowel and 'a' before most words which begin with a consonant.

Write 'a' or 'an' in the spaces.

_____ engine   _____ clock   _____ table   _____ frog

_____ light   _____ island   _____ door   _____ arch

_____ octopus   _____ umbrella

3

✿ Circle 'a' or 'an' to complete the sentences.

1. This is (a, an) old painting.

2. I have (a, an) new umbrella.

3. That is (a, an) ugly building.

4. Barbados is (a, an) small island.

5. Mummy bought (a, an) iron.

6. He has (a, an) swollen ankle.

7. She ate (a, an) apple, (a, an) banana and (a, an) orange.

8. We saw (a, an) ostrich, (a, an) eagle and (a, an) swan.

❀ Call the words in the box. Now, circle the word if the 'u' at the beginning of the word says its name or sounds like the word 'you'.

united	usual	uproar	ugly	union
uphill	uniform	untidy	utensil	uncle
useful	under	unit	unhappy	unable

❀ We use 'a' before words which begin with 'u' when the 'u' says its name. We use 'an' before the other words which begin with 'u'.

❀ Write 'a' or 'an' before these words.

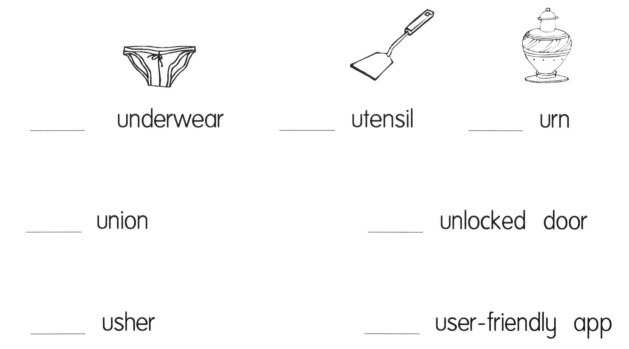

_____ underwear   _____ utensil   _____ urn

_____ union   _____ unlocked door

_____ usher   _____ user-friendly app

✿ **Complete the sentences with 'a' or 'an'.**

1. I have _____ uncle who lives in St. James.

2. A fingernail clip is _____ useful tool.

3. She carried _____ umbrella and a coat.

4. Mummy ironed _____ uniform for me.

5. _____ unicorn is not a real animal.

6. _____ usher showed me to my seat.

7. A pound is _____ unit of weight.

8. _____ union is an organization of workers.

❀ When the letter 'h' at the beginning of a word is not pronounced it is said to be silent. Call the words in the box and circle them if the 'h' is silent.

hour	horse	happy	heir	hungry
hammer	honour	hold	honest	hard

❀ We use 'an' before words which begin with a silent 'h' and 'a' before words which do not begin with a silent 'h'.

❀ Write 'a' or 'an' before these words.

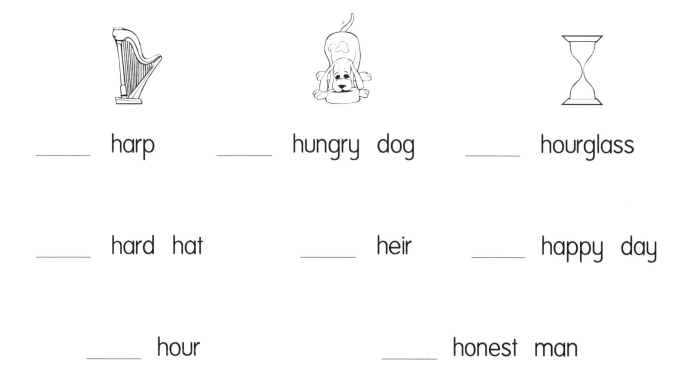

_____ harp   _____ hungry dog   _____ hourglass

_____ hard hat   _____ heir   _____ happy day

_____ hour   _____ honest man

✿ **Complete the sentences with 'a' or 'an'.**

1. He is _____ honest boy.

2. _____ hexagon has six sides.

3. They waited half _____ hour for their lunch.

4. She is _____ happy girl.

5. The prisoner was put in _____ holding cell.

6. He is _____ honour student.

7. The king wanted _____ heir to his throne.

8. Daddy bought _____ hammer from _____ hardware store.

✿ Write a <u>suitable</u> word to complete each sentence.

1. Did Daddy buy an _____ _____ from the van?

2. Will you give a _____ to your teacher?

3. They bought a _____ from the shop.

4. She has an _____ book to give you.

5. Mother hates an _____ room.

✿ Complete the story using 'a' or 'an'.

We waited ____ hour for the bus. The

driver said there was ____ accident with

____ blue car and ____ orange truck. I

took ____ seat beside ____ old man.

He told me ____ interesting story about

____ woman who wanted to carry ____

animal on ____ bus.

Section 2

Nouns

- things
- animals
- persons
- places

❀ In the boxes above the nouns in the story write:

        'A' for animal,   'Pl' for place

        'T' for thing,   'Pe' for person/s.

The children walked to the beach with Mummy and their dog. They passed the supermarket and a church. Mummy carried a bag with cake and drinks. At the beach, they saw Daddy selling fish and lobsters.

❀ Now write the nouns in the correct boxes.

Animal

Place

Thing

Person

11

✿ The names of things are called nouns. Sort these nouns in the correct boxes.

hammer	rose	carrot	pizza	drill
saw	knife	sunflower	grapefruit	daisy
pasta	lily	scissors	hibiscus	dumpling

Nouns (things)

Tools	Flowers	Foods

✿ Write the missing letters for these nouns.

__r__ck   __h__in   t__bl__

✤ **Underline the nouns which name <u>things</u> in each sentence.**

1. I use milk with cereal.

2. Are there pencils in the case?

3. My shoes have blue laces.

4. Did you put the fruits in the fridge?

5. Some water is in the bucket.

6. Are the flowers in the vase?

7. The knives and forks have been washed.

8. Ripe coconuts are in the tree.

9. Some snacks are in the cupboard.

10. Did you clean the chairs and tables?

✿ The names of animals are called nouns. Sort these nouns in the correct boxes.

dove	tortoise	shark	sparrow	crocodile
iguana	goldfish	lizard	flamingo	snapper
owl	salmon	snake	penguin	flying fish

Nouns (animals)

Birds	Fishes	Reptiles

✿ Unscramble the words for these nouns.

atb   abre   wleah

_____   _____   _____

❀ **Underline the nouns which name <u>animals</u> in each sentence.**

1. Lizards eat flies.

2. A whale is not a fish.

3. Is a cheetah faster than a tiger?

4. An elephant is larger than a horse.

5. Are toads different from frogs?

6. The ewe had two lambs.

7. Some ants and bees work very hard.

8. The sow and her ten piglets are in that pen.

9. Horses and ponies look similar.

10. The ducks and swans swim on the lake.

✿ **Complete each sentence with a suitable noun.**

1. The meat from a _____ is called pork.

2. The _____ flew from the hive.

3. A _____ is the mother of a kitten.

4. Can you hear the _____ chirping in the tree?

5. Beef is the meat from a _____ .

6. The _____ growled at the postman.

7. A baby sheep is called a _____ .

8. A den is the home for a _____ .

9. An _____ is a tiny animal.

10. A _____ is a baby whale, elephant or cow.

✿ Words which name persons are called nouns. Sort these nouns in the correct boxes.

sister	footballer	teacher	farmer	watchman
uncle	cricketer	father	plumber	grandmother
cousin	shoemaker	surfer	jockey	gymnast

Nouns (persons)

Sportsmen	Family Members	Community Workers

✿ Match the nouns to the pictures.

librarian   priest   surgeon   cook

✿ **Underline the nouns which name <u>persons</u> in each sentence.**

1. My brother is older than my sister.

2. The nurse is taking care of the patients.

3. Is the carpenter working on the house?

4. Carl fixes a car in the garage.

5. The priest spoke to the congregation.

6. The students listened to their teacher.

7. Ben takes the tourists to St. Lawrence Gap.

8. The bartender made cocktails.

9. Did the principal discipline the children?

10. Her mother and father got married in June.

✿ **Complete each sentence with a suitable noun from the box.**

> fisherman, athlete, uncle, postman, cashier, farmer

1. The _____ won two races.

2. Did that _____ check your groceries?

3. The _____ caught many dolphins.

4. My father's brother is my _____.

5. The _____ sold vegetables to the hotel.

6. Did the _____ deliver the mail?

✿ **Write the names for these pictures.**

> singer,   dancer,   drummer,   guitarist

_____   _____   _____   _____

✿ The names of places are called nouns. Sort these nouns in the correct boxes.

Grenada	Rock Hall	Apes Hill	Oistins
Trinidad	England	Bay Street	Warrens
Holetown	India	St. Vincent	Bridgetown
Halls Road	Castries	Speightstown	

Nouns (places)

Countries	Roads\Districts	Cities\Towns

✿ **Underline the nouns which name <u>places</u> in each sentence.**

1. She lives in Antigua.

2. She visited her friend in the hospital.

3. They played cricket on the pasture.

4. I will meet my aunt in Oistins.

5. We had a picnic at the beach.

6. He walks to school every day.

7. Shall we go to Bridgetown?

8. The farmer planted okras in his garden.

9. Was the fair held in the park?

10. My Daddy works in Wildey.

✿ **Complete each sentence with a suitable noun from the box.**

stadium	post office	library	beach	hospital
airport	restaurant	school	farm	supermarket

1. The planes landed at the _____.

2. The children made sandcastles at the _____.

3. Are the athletes going to the _____?

4. At the _____, we buy groceries.

5. The food at that _____ is tasty.

6. Have you taken the letters to the _____?

7. At _____, we learn many things.

8. We saw animals and plants on the _____.

9. Did you borrow two books from the _____?

10. When Grandma broke her arm, we took her to the _____.

✿ **Nouns are names of things, animals, persons, and places. Write 'N' above the nouns in the sentences.**

                  N   N

Example: Cats like to drink milk.

1. Many shoppers were buying gifts.

2. You should wear your helmet when riding your bike.

3. We get medicine from the pharmacy.

4. The horses were in the paddock.

5. Were the fans annoyed with the players?

6. A hare is faster than a tortoise.

7. The wind caused the fire to spread quickly.

8. Did the parade take place in the city?

9. The butcher worked in the abattoir.

10. Did the mongoose kill the snake?

Section 3

Plurals

- most nouns
- nouns ending in 'ch' and 'sh'
- nouns ending in 's' and 'ss'
- nouns ending in 'x' and 'z'
- irregular nouns
- nouns which do not change
- nouns ending in 'o'
- nouns ending in 'y'
- nouns ending in 'f' and 'fe'
- nouns existing in plural form

✽ We add 's' to most singular nouns to make them plural. Make these nouns plural. Call the words that you have written.

horse

drill

mongoose

_____

_____

_____

desk

mask

text

_____

_____

_____

vest

fist

tourist

_____

_____

_____

✿ We add 'es' to singular nouns to make them plural when they end with 'ch'. Make these singular nouns plural and write them in the spaces.

Singular (one)   **Plural** (more than one)

watch   two   _watches_

match   some   _____

torch   those   _____

church   most   _____

peach   these   _____

sandwich   several   _____

branch   many   _____

bench   a few   _____

✤ **Write the plural form of the correct noun in each space.**

Example:

You cleaned one bench but I cleaned four <u>benches</u>.

1. Has he built one hutch or two _____?

2. If you buy a bunch, I shall buy two _____.

3. His cut took one stitch but mine took four _____.

4. Is he walking with one crutch or two _____?

5. Only one coach came to our school but two _____ went to theirs.

6. Did they dig a trench or three _____?

7. I took a catch and the wicketkeeper took four _____.

8. They won one cricket match but we won all of our _____.

9. The groundsmen prepared one pitch but the field has three _____.

✿ We add 'es' to singular nouns to make them plural when they end with 'sh'. Make these singular nouns plural and complete the puzzle.

Down   1 dash   2 fish   3 flash   4 brush

Across   5 sash   6 eyelash   7 lash   8 crash

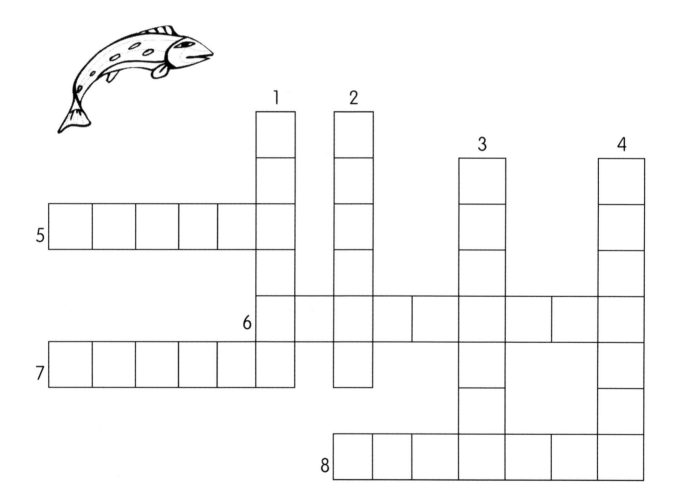

❀ Write the plurals for these nouns.

bush   toothbrush   crash   flash

_____   _____   _____   _____

❀ Make the noun in the brackets plural and write it in the space.

1. He painted the sea in _____ of blue.
   (splash)

2. May I share the _____ ? (paintbrush)

3. The child was given three _____ . (wish)

4. Is her skin full of _____ ? (rash)

5. After dinner, we had to wash many _____ .
   (dish)

6. Did you get the _____ ? (sash)

✾ **Make the noun in the brackets plural and write it in the space.**

1. Three _____ are in the aquarium. (fish)

2. She waters her _____ daily. (plant)

3. Twelve _____ were in the regatta. (sailboat)

4. Did the boy get _____ from his mother? (lash)

5. Yesterday, we planted cucumber _____. (seed)

6. We ate cheese _____ for lunch. (sandwich)

7. Many _____ fell from the plum trees.
   (branch)

8. The _____ were closed on Good Friday.
   (store)

9. The _____ were cleared this morning. (bush)

10. The _____ were placed in three rows.
    (bench)

✿ Most singular nouns which end with 's' and 'ss' are made plural by adding 'es'. Make these singular nouns plural.

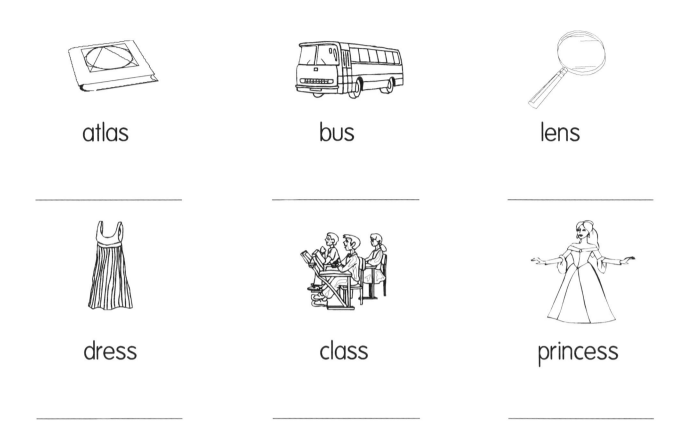

atlas

bus

lens

_____

_____

_____

dress

class

princess

_____

_____

_____

✿ Write the singular or the plural for the nouns.

Singular	Plural	Singular	Plural
1. cross _____		3._____ viruses	
2. plus _____		4._____ bosses	

❀ Most singular nouns which end with 'x' and 'z' are made plural by adding 'es'. Make these singular nouns plural.

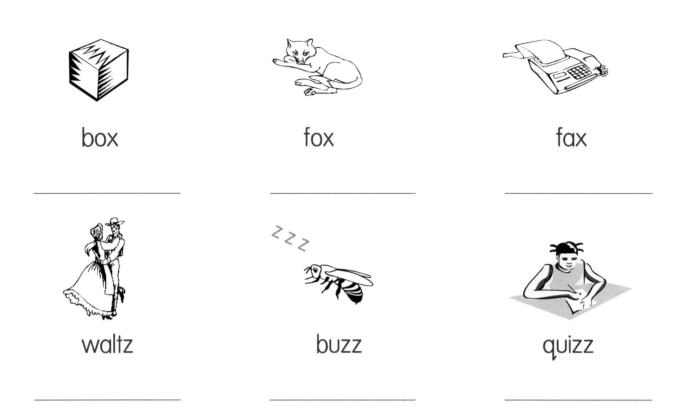

box

_____

fox

_____

fax

_____

waltz

_____

buzz

_____

quizz

_____

❀ Write the singular or the plural for the nouns.

Singular	Plural		Singular	Plural
1. quartz	_____		3. _____	topazes
2. wax	_____		4. _____	mixes

32

Some nouns change to form their plurals. Complete the plurals below by writing the missing vowels. Then copy each word.

Singular Nouns	Plural Nouns							Copy
louse	l	i	c	e				lice
foot	f		t					
tooth	t		t	h				
goose	g		s					
man	m		n					
woman	w		m	n				
die	d		c					
child	c	h		l	d	r	n	
ox		x		n				
mouse	m		c					

Write the word for each picture.

_____   _____   _____

33

✿ **Make the noun in the brackets plural and write it in the space.**

1. The _____ played volleyball. (man)

2. Many _____ were in Queen's Park. (child)

3. The shoes were hurting my _____.(foot)

4. The _____ scurried about the dump. (mouse)

5. The dentist examined my _____. (tooth)

6. I saw some _____ in the pond. (goose)

7. The _____ were shopping in the mall.
   (woman)

8. We played a game with _____. (die)

9. The _____ were grazing in the field. (ox)

10. Flies, bugs and _____ are insects. (louse)

✿ The nouns in the box have their singular and plural forms the same. Circle them in the puzzle.

| salmon | aircraft | cannon | trout | offspring |
| corn | sheep | swine | deer | moose |

```
s  y  e  e  t  s  h  e  e  p  n  u
a  o  e  t  r  o  u  t  d  t  z  e
l  c  c  g  z  t  h  i  c  d  x  d
m  e  a  i  r  c  r  a  f  t  u  e
o  n  n  v  m  l  d  c  t  d  n  e
n  a  n  r  o  b  r  o  o  n  o  r
f  b  o  a  o  n  n  r  o  c  h  c
r  k  n  q  s  w  i  n  e  f  p  s
o  e  b  z  e  v  e  l  e  r  t  r
u  r  o  f  f  s  p  r  i  n  g  q
```

✿ **Write the plural of the noun, in the brackets, in the space.**

1. The farmer sold six black belly _____. (sheep)

2. We saw some _____ at the zoo. (moose)

3. Several _____ swam down the river. (salmon)

4. A hangar is a place where _____ are kept. (aircraft)

5. Do you buy roast _____ by the roadside? (corn)

6. Pigs are _____. (swine)

7. Those _____ have long antlers. (deer)

8. Mother bought some _____ from the fish market. (trout)

9. Some old _____ are at the Garrison Savannah. (cannon)

✿ Some singular nouns which end with 'o' are made plural by adding 's'. Make these singular nouns plural and complete the puzzle.

1. piano   2. zero   3. radio   4. photo   5. zoo

6. patio   7. video   8. avocado

1 ☐☐☐☐☐☐

2 ☐☐☐☐☐

3 ☐☐☐☐☐☐

4 ☐☐☐☐☐☐

5 ☐☐☐☐

6 ☐☐☐☐☐☐

7 ☐☐☐☐☐☐

8 ☐☐☐☐☐☐☐☐

✿ Some singular nouns which end with 'o' are made plural by adding 'es'. Write the correct word in each space.

Singular (one)   **Plural** (more than one)

potato   some _____

mango   four _____

_____   these tomatoes

mosquito   some _____

_____   a few echoes

hero   ten _____

volcano   two _____

_____   many banjoes

buffalo   those _____

✿ **Write the plural of the noun, in the brackets, in the space.**

1. I took some _____ of the displays. (photo)

2. Some _____ carry diseases. (mosquito)

3. I prefer _____ to oranges. (avocado)

4. The music _____ were entertaining. (video)

5. The ripe _____ were used to make ketchup. (tomato)

✿ **Cross out each incorrect noun and write the correct noun on the line.**

Example: The church has a grand pianoes. <u>piano</u>

1. Barbados had ten national heros. _____

2. Mangos were sold for one dollar. _____

3. We saw many animals at the two zooes. _____

4. I like to eat sweet potatos. _____

5. Five take away five is zeros. _____

�֍ Circle the noun if a vowel comes just before the 'y'.

baby	boy	day	daisy	fly	turkey
story	tray	poppy	pony	toy	donkey

Now sort the nouns in the correct boxes.

Vowel just before the 'y'	Consonant just before the 'y'
monkey	lady

✿ Nouns which end with 'y' and have a vowel just before the 'y' form their plurals by adding 's'. Write the correct word in each space.

Singular (one)   **Plural** (more than one)

boy   some _____

jay   four _____

_____   these strays

_____   a few guys

toy   two _____

valley   some _____

_____   many alleys

41

✾ **Make the noun in the brackets plural and write it in the space.**

1. They are two _____ to my home. (way)

2. Those dogs are _____. (stray)

3. There are seven _____ in one week. (day)

4. Mary lost a bunch of _____. (key)

5. _____ are fishes with flat bodies. (Stingray)

6. Four children have _____ in February. (birthday)

7. The servers washed the _____. (tray)

8. Two green _____ were in the tree. (monkey)

9. The _____ from the sun are very bright. (ray)

10. Did the _____ put away the _____?
       (boy)   (toy)

✤ Nouns which end with 'y' and have a consonant just before the 'y' form their plurals by:

     (**a**) changing the 'y' to 'i'   (**b**) adding 'es'

Example: cherry   →   cherri   →   cherri**es**

✤ Make these nouns plural.

Singular Nouns	Change 'y' to 'i'	Plural Nouns Add 'es'
berry	berri	berri**es**
sky		
army		
spy		
ferry		
lolly		
duty		

✤ **Make the nouns in the brackets plural and complete each sentence.**

1. The _____ are going to church. (lady)

2. Many _____ were in this garden. (daisy)

3. Did you ride the _____ at the fair? (pony)

4. Daddy reads us bedtime _____. (story)

5. The _____ escaped from the cage. (bunny)

6. We must go home to our _____. (family)

7. The _____ swarmed the dead animal. (fly)

8. Mummy bought _____ for the cake. (cherry)

9. She works taking care of _____. (baby)

10. We got _____ when we donated money. (poppy)

✿ We add 's' to some singular nouns to make them plural when they end with 'f' or 'fe'. Make these singular nouns plural and complete the puzzle.

1. dwarf   2. safe   3. chef   4. chief   5. handkerchief

6. roof   7. gulf   8. muff   9. proof

1 ⬚⬚⬚⬚⬚⬚   6 ⬚⬚⬚⬚⬚

2 ⬚⬚⬚⬚⬚   7 ⬚⬚⬚⬚

3 ⬚⬚⬚⬚   8 ⬚⬚⬚⬚

4 ⬚⬚⬚⬚⬚   9 ⬚⬚⬚⬚⬚⬚

5 ⬚⬚⬚⬚⬚⬚⬚⬚⬚⬚⬚⬚⬚⬚

✿ Some nouns which end with 'fe' or 'f' form their plurals by:

(a) changing the 'f' or 'fe' to 'v'   (b) adding 'es'

Example: calf   →   calv   →   calv**es**

✿ Make these nouns plural.

Singular Nouns		Plural Nouns
	Change 'f' or 'fe' to 'v'	Add 'es'
life	liv	liv**es**
hoof		
wife		
knife		
scarf		
self		
loaf		

❁ **Make the noun in the brackets plural and write it in the space.**

1. We cut the oranges in ____________. (half)
2. I read the story of 'The ____________ and the Shoemaker'. (Elf)
3. The ____________ are cooking in the restaurant. (chef)
4. The maid cleaned the dirty ____________. (shelf)
5. Many ____________ fell from the soursop tree. (leaf)
6. I have many ________________. (handkerchief)
7. Daddy buys two ____________ of bread. (loaf)
8. Did you read 'Snow White and the Seven ____________'? (Dwarf)
9. Many Barbadians have solar panels on their ____________. (roof)
10. Mummy bought a set of ____________. (knife)

✾ **The nouns in the box exist only in the plural form. Circle them in the puzzle.**

tweezers	innings	tights	tongs
binoculars	shorts	pants	manners
fireworks	pliers	jeans	series

s	m	v	f	n	a	p	l	i	e	r	s
j	a	w	s	e	r	i	e	s	z	j	c
t	n	f	k	m	p	s	q	s	s	f	b
i	n	n	i	n	g	s	x	h	b	c	i
g	e	t	e	y	l	y	j	o	i	h	n
h	r	t	w	e	e	z	e	r	s	r	o
t	s	j	f	x	w	x	i	t	s	l	c
s	y	e	p	a	n	t	s	s	o	v	u
j	a	a	e	a	u	q	d	p	r	h	l
s	h	n	d	b	t	o	n	g	s	w	a
b	q	s	h	m	i	h	v	t	o	q	r
x	f	i	r	e	w	o	r	k	s	t	s

48

✿ **Complete the sentences with these plural nouns.**

spectacles	clothes	pajamas	scissors
headphones	innings	stairs	goggles

1. Use the _____ to cut the string.

2. Did you wear your pink _____ to bed?

3. Grandma cannot see without her _____.

4. Use the _____ to listen to the music.

5. I wear _____ when I go swimming.

6. She did not know what _____ to wear.

7. Do not run on the _____.

8. Barbados made two hundred and thirty runs in their second _____.

✿ **Write the plural of the words.**

pan	fish	roof
___	___	___
man	stitch	hoof
___	___	___

box	house	goose
___	___	___
ox	mouse	moose
___	___	___

boot	pie	booth
___	___	___
foot	die	tooth
___	___	___

✿ Make the words plural and write them in the correct place.

book	man	corn	mango	table	sheep
quizz	ox	bus	mongoose	foot	moose

Add 's'			

Add 'es'			

Change the Word			

Word does not Change			

✿ Make the nouns in the brackets plural and complete each sentence.

1. We were told not to throw _____. (stone)

2. Barbados has many beautiful _____. (beach)

3. The _____ were playing hopscotch. (child)

4. Many _____ are on the runway. (aircraft)

51

✿ **Cross out each plural noun and write the singular noun above it.**

                                maid   floor

Example: The ~~maids~~ cleaned the ~~floors~~.

1. Will the girls walk the dogs?

2. Please put the brushes by the paints.

3. The men sharpened the cutlasses.

4. Did the cats catch the mice?

5. The mosquitoes buzzed in my ears.

6. Did the ladies buy the turkeys?

7. The dwarfs could not reach the high shelves.

8. Can the children play on the swings?

9. The sheep ate the mangoes.

✿ Write the nouns in their plural forms in the correct place.

lady	clothes	shelf	fairy	stairs	story
loaf	tongs	roof	chimney	piano	leaf

Add 's'			

Change the 'y' to 'i' and add 'es'			

Change the 'f' to 'v' and add 'es'			

Word is Always Plural			

✿ Complete each sentence with the plural form of the noun in the brackets.

1. The _____ are playing cricket. (boy)

2. Those _____ are made of silk. (scarf)

3. The _____ were resting under the tree. (deer)

4. I lost a pair of _____ yesterday. (binoculars)

✻ **Rewrite the sentences and change the <u>singular nouns</u> to <u>plural nouns</u>.**

1. Will the man paint the roof?

_____

2. The jockey whipped the horse.

_____

3. The baby cried in the crib.

_____

4. Did the woman buy shorts?

_____

5. I bought the battery for the torch.

_____

6. Did the thief steal the radio?

_____

7. The maid washed the glass and the dish.

_____

Section 4

Verbs

am, is, are

was, were

has, have

✽ **We use the word 'am' when we are speaking about ourselves. Write 'am' in the spaces.**

1. I _____ at school.

2. I _____ sitting at my desk.

3. I _____ writing in my grammar book.

4. I _____ hoping to get all of my work correct.

✽ **Write five sentences about yourself using 'am'.
The word 'I' is always a capital letter.**

1. _____

    Say who you are.

2. _____

    Say how old you are.

3. _____

    Say if you are tall or short.

4. _____

    Say what class you are in.

5. _____

    Say how you feel.

✿ Write these words correctly under singular or plural.

| we | this | she | they | that | you |
| those | he | these | I | it | some |

Singular

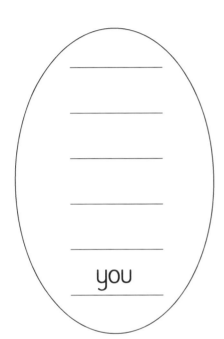

you

Plural

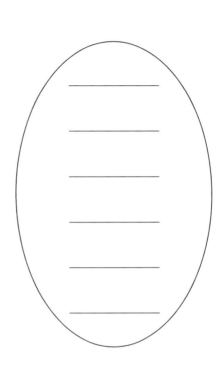

✿ Choose a suitable word from above to write in each space.

1. _____ cherries

2. _____ glass

3. _____ mangoes

4. _____ pram

5. _____ women

✿ We use the word 'is' when we speak about singular words and 'are' when we speak about plural words. We always use 'are' with the word 'you'.

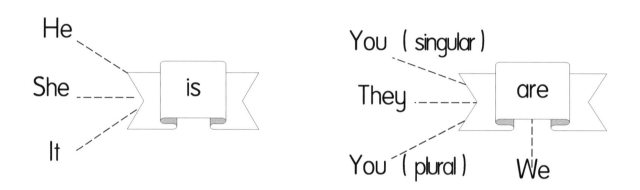

✿ **Circle 'is' or 'are' to complete the sentences.**

1. (Is, Are) you going to Bridgetown Market?

2. (Is, Are) it too far to walk?

3. We (is, are) waiting for the bus.

4. They (is, are) jumping in the band.

5. She (is, are) buying fish cakes.

⊛ Complete the tables by putting 'am', 'is' or 'are' in the spaces.

That game	
A sheep	
Some churches	
Both classes	
The cassava	
An egret	
I	
We	
This tooth	
Those plants	
He	
The reefs	

Every car	
Another player	
These stories	
Daniel and I	
You	
A calf	
Each pupil	
Jan and Roy	
Neither boy	
Six roast corn	
Either bus	
They	

Write 'am', 'is' or 'are' in the spaces.

1. Every door _____ open.

2. That player _____ very good.

3. Some classes _____ big.

4. Those stories _____ interesting.

5. I _____ going to St. Andrew.

6. Each child _____ going on the school tour.

7. A few roofs _____ being repaired.

8. Several mice _____ on the trap.

9. Neither singer _____ performing.

10. Jana and Mia _____ smiling.

❀ **Rewrite these sentences to make them plural.**

Examples: Here (is) the (cup.)

Here are the cups.

The (boy) (is) eating.

The boys are eating.

1. The girl is playing.

_____

2. Here is the pencil.

_____

3. Is the desk clean?

_____

4. Is the man in the van?

_____

5. The lens is on the table.

_____

❀ We use the word 'was' when we speak about singular words and 'were' when we speak about plural words. We always use 'were' with the word 'you'.

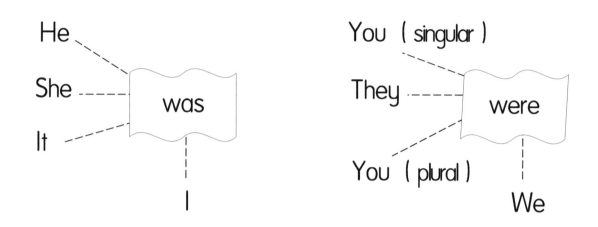

He
She
It
was
I

You (singular)
They
were
You (plural)
We

❀ Circle 'was' or 'were' to complete the sentences.

1. He (was, were) writing a story.

2. (Was, Were) you in the lunchroom?

3. They (was, were) fixing puzzles.

4. It (was, were) not in my bag.

5. Jada and I (was, were) running for the van.

✿ **Complete the tables correctly with 'was' or 'were'.**

He			A monkey	
A maid			The surfers	

Kim and Paul			Most beaches	
That edoe			We	

The doctor			I	
Some stoves			Mary and I	

✿ **Write 'was' or 'were' in the spaces.**

1. They _____ told to give of their best.

2. She _____ surfing at Bathsheba in St. Joseph.

3. I _____ watching the news on C.B.C.

4. Carl and Karen _____ playing road tennis.

5. _____ the children making kites?

6. It _____ a lovely day at the Garrison.

63

✿ **Rewrite these sentences to make them plural.**

Example: Where (was) the (marble)?

Where were the marbles?

1. The cat was sleeping.

_____

2. Where was the book?

_____

3. Was the room untidy?

_____

4. The mango was placed in the bin.

_____

5. The child was on the swing.

_____

❀ We use the word 'has' when we speak about singular words and 'have' when we speak about plural words. We always use 'have' with the words 'you' and 'I'.

❀ Write the words in the box on the correct lines.

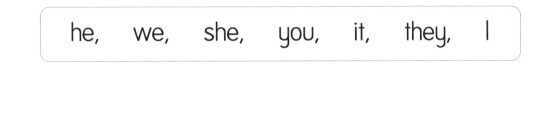

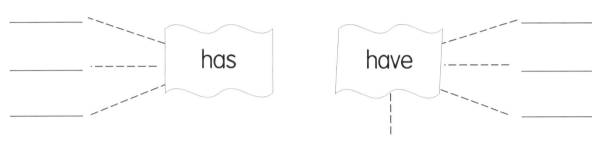

❀ **Circle 'has' or 'have' in the brackets.**

1. Where (has, have) you been?

2. Do they (has, have) many tickets?

3. I (has, have) to go to bed early.

4. She (has, have) already eaten.

5. It (has, have) been a long time.

✿ **Complete the sentences with 'has' or 'have'.**

Pip   Troy   Sheena   Pam   Sara

1. _____ the dog a bone?

2. Yes, it _____ a bone.

3. _____ Troy a toy truck?

4. He _____ a toy truck.

5. Troy, Sheena and I _____ toys.

6. We _____ toys.

7. _____ Pam and Sara any dolls?

8. They _____ dolls.

9. _____ you any toys?

10. Yes, I _____ toys.

66

✾ **Rewrite the sentences to make them plural.**

Example: The (dog) (has) the (bone.)

   The dogs have the bones.

1. The girl has the red ball.

_____

2. The bird has flown from the tree.

_____

3. Where has the boy gone?

_____

4. The glass has been broken.

_____

5. My daughter has the package.

_____

✿ **Choose a word from the box to complete the sentences.**

am, is, are, was, were, has, have

1. She _____ a fair person.

2. I _____ six years old today.

3. _____ they playing marble cricket yesterday?

4. He _____ going to the concert but it was cancelled.

5. _____ you been to Miami?

6. We _____ taking care of the children last night.

7. _____ we going home now?

8. When the rain fell, I _____ sleeping.

9. Mother _____ flying fish and cou-cou for lunch.

10. Yesterday, Kim and Dave _____ playing dominoes.

Section 5

Capital Letters

- days of the week
- months of the year
- names of persons
- names of places
- names of animals
- holidays/festivals
- brands
- other

✾ **The days of the week and months of the year always begin with a capital letter. Write these days and months correctly.**

tuesday   monday   wednesday

_____   _____   _____

august   january   march

_____   _____   _____

✾ **Cross out the nouns that are written incorrectly and write them correctly on the lines.**

1. My party is on friday. _____

2. On saturday, I went to church. _____

3. My little sister was born in april. _____

4. We celebrate Independence in november. _____

5. This year, may has four sundays. _____ _____

6. The first wednesday in february is my birthday.

_____   _____

✿ The table shows what Mummy gave Jan to drink during the week.

sunday	monday	tuesday	wednesday	thursday	friday	saturday
Sorrel Drink	Mauby	Tamarind Drink	Water	Tomato Drink	Fruit Punch	Soursop Punch

✿ Write the days correctly to complete the sentences

1. Jan drank tamarind drink on _____.

2. On _____, she drank mauby.

3. Soursop punch was given to her on _____.

4. _____ was the day when she had water.

5. Jan liked _____ because fruit punch is her favourite drink.

6. On _____, tomato drink was given to her.

7. Jan enjoyed the sorrel on _____.

❀ **Write the months correctly to complete the sentences.**

january
february
march
april
may
june
july
august
september
october
november
december

1. My birthday is in ______________.

2. The first month is ______________.

3. ______________ and ______________ begin with the letter 'm'.

4. June comes just before ______________.

5. ______________ comes just after July.

6. The month between January and March is ______________.

7. The last month of the year is ______________.

✿ **Write these sentences correctly. Remember to write a capital letter for the day and the month.**

1. We take fruits to school on fridays.

_____

2. may is called Child Month.

_____

3. The new year starts in january.

_____

4. tuesday comes after monday.

_____

5. Our summer vacation is in july and august.

_____

6. The weekend falls on saturday and sunday.

_____

7. What date is the second thursday in october?

_____

❀ The names of people always begin with a capital letter. Write these names correctly.

miss greene

_____

dr. roberts

_____

mrs. kinch

_____

mr. brian talma

_____

dame nita barrow

_____

sir grantley adams

_____

❀ Write these sentences correctly.

1. Is her name sandy or mandy?

_____

2. Are danny and kayla brother and sister?

_____

3. I saw carl burke in Bridgetown.

_____

✿ **Always begin the names of places with a capital letter. Complete the sentences correctly with these places of interest in Barbados.**

garrison	kensington oval	cherry tree hill
bathsheba	flower forest	harrison's cave

1. Cricket is played at _____.

2. We can watch horse racing at the _____.

3. Do you go surfing at _____?

4. There is a waterfall in _____.

5. There are many beautiful flowers at the _____

    _____.

6. Did you see the view from _____

    _____?

✸ **The names of parishes begin with a capital letter. Write these correctly.**

st. philip   st. lucy   christ church

_____   _____   _____

✸ **Write these sentences correctly. Remember to begin the name of each place and person with a capital letter.**

1. lara went to miami.

_____

2. Does sharon work in st. michael?

_____

3. mr. cox drove to st. peter.

_____

4. Is fred going to st. john tomorrow?

_____

5. The capital of barbados is bridgetown.

_____

6. kendra lives in greens, st. george.

_____

7. i took a bus from speightstown to holetown.

_____

❀ **Always begin the names of pets with a capital letter. Write these sentences correctly.**

1. Joe named his puppies bumba and diva.

____

2. The donkey, molly, delivered the last canes.

____

3. My pet fishes are flipper and holly.

____

4. Sara named her kittens peach and roxie.

____

❀ **The names of special days and festivals begin with a capital letter. Write these correctly.**

easter   christmas   kadooment day

__________   __________   __________

good friday   father's day

__________   __________

✿ The table shows the months in which some holidays are celebrated in Barbados. The names of holidays always begin with a capital letter.

Months	Holidays
January	*errol barrow day*
April	*national heroes day*
May	*labour day*
August	*emancipation day*
November	*independence day*
December	*christmas day*

✿ Write the holidays correctly to complete the sentences.

1. In August, we celebrate _____ .

2. _____ is celebrated in January.

3. On the 28th April, we celebrate _____ .

4. _____ is the 1st of May.

5. December 25th is _____ .

6. On November 30th, Barbados celebrates _____ .

✿ The names of brands usually begin with a capital letter. Write these brands correctly.

farmer's choice

solar dynamics

_____

_____

bajan pride

sprite

_____

_____

✿ The special names of nouns begin with a capital letter. Write these sentences correctly.

1. Our school has *cub scouts* and *brownies*.

_____

2. My sister can speak *french* and *spanish*.

_____

3. Have you ever been to *illaro court* ?

_____

4. The van delivered *pinehill* juices and *bico* ice cream.

_____

✿ Each word of titles of poems, songs, books, newspapers and shows usually begins with a capital letter.
Write these titles correctly.

the barbados advocate   grammar made easy

_____   _____

✿ Write these sentences correctly.

1. My favourite nursery rhyme is 'humpty dumpty'.

_____

2. My sister watches 'sesame street' on evenings.

_____

3. 'umbrella', by Rihanna, was a popular song.

_____

4. 'bim i love you' was written by Red Plastic Bag.

_____

5. Dad reads 'the daily nation' newspaper every day.

_____

6. I like to read 'the gingerbread man'.

_____

✿ **Write these sentences correctly.**

1. We went to oistins last friday night.

_____

2. sir garfield sobers is a famous cricketer.

_____

3. My favourite book is 'thumbelina'.

_____

4. pam and i were born in november.

_____

5. Where is baxters road?

_____

6. We will shop in bridgetown on saturday.

_____

7. have you seen my cat, ross?

_____

8. We fly our kites on easter sunday.

_____

Section 6

Opposites

Prefixes

Homophones

Compound Words

Alphabetical Order

Synonyms

✤ The pictures show opposites. Write the word for each.

soft	sharp	dark
hard	dull	light
easy	bright	heavy

_____   _____   _____   _____

_____   _____   _____   _____

      26+15=   2+2=

_____   _____   _____   _____

✾ **Write the opposite of the word in <u>bold</u> to complete each sentence.**

1. This knife was too **dull** to cut the meat so I used the _____ one.

2. We cannot see well with the _____ light, so turn on the **bright** one.

3. A rock is **hard** but cotton is _____.

4. The first sum was **easy** but the second one was _____.

5. The chair is **light** but the table is _____.

6. Daddy bought a _____-blue shirt and a **dark**-blue pants.

7. The boats tossed in the **rough** sea but sailed smoothly on the _____ sea.

8. A soursop feels _____ but a mango feels **smooth**.

❀ **Complete each sentence with the opposite of the word in the brackets.**

1. My home is _____ from the school. (near)

2. I have a _____, pretty pencil. (short)

3. They went (inside) but we remained _____.

4. Did you cut a _____ slice of bread? (thick)

5. They had to _____ the building. (enter)

6. The swing goes (backward) and _____.

7. Danny came _____ in the race. (last)

8. This painting is very _____. (ugly)

9. We wrote the _____ of the nouns. (singular)

10. The (rich) man gave money to the _____ beggar.

✿ Shade the circle to show the opposite of the word in <u>bold</u> in each line. The first one is done for you.

1. **full** ○ there ● empty ○ half ○ far

2. **war** ○ peace ○ pace ○ tar ○ wake

3. **clean** ○ dry ○ close ○ dirty ○ class

4. **less** ○ little ○ more ○ long ○ many

5. **above** ○ high ○ about ○ behind ○ below

6. **alive** ○ away ○ dead ○ awake ○ dark

7. **low** ○ bottom ○ long ○ high ○ under

8. **given** ○ gave ○ taken ○ give ○ took

9. **floating** ○ flake ○ flying ○ sinking ○ soaking

10. **horizontal** ○ horizon ○ zone ○ very ○ vertical

❀ A prefix is added to the front of a word to change its meaning. Some opposites are formed by putting the prefix 'un' in front of the word. The prefix 'un' means not.

❀ Form opposites of the words in brackets to fill each space.

Example:

1. (packed) __unpacked__   2. (kind) _____

3. (cooked) _____   4. (afraid) _____

5. (block) _____   6. (paid) _____

7. Did you _____ the door? (lock)

8. The room is _____, so put away the toys. (tidy)

9. Mia is _____ because she lost her pet. (happy)

10. When will you _____ your present? (wrap)

11. Adam was _____ to complete the race. (able)

12. Micah was _____, so he went to the doctor. (well)

✿ Some opposites are formed by putting the prefix 'dis' in front of the word. The prefix 'dis' means not.

✿ Form opposites of the words in brackets to fill each space.

Example:

1. (agree) __**dis**agree__

2. (able) _____

3. (close) _____

4. (approve) _____

5. (belief) _____

6. (qualified) _____

7. I _____ when it rains on games day. (like)

8. People who steal are _____. (honest)

9. Children should never be _____. (respectful)

10. Smoking is _____ in public places. (allowed)

11. The match was _____ because of bad weather. (continued)

12. Do not _____ the school rules. (obey)

✿ **Add either the prefix 'dis' or 'un' to each word in the brackets to form opposites. Complete the sentences with the words formed.**

1. Children buy too many _____ snacks. (healthy)

2. The jockey _____ the horse. (mounts)

3. The magician made the dove _____. (appear)

4. The man _____ his pit-bull. (tied)

5. Harry is always _____ for class. (prepared)

6. I _____ leafy vegetables. (like)

7. The meat is _____. (cooked)

8. It was _____ to treat her that way. (fair)

9. I felt _____ in the hard bed. (comfortable)

10. My mother hates an _____ room. (tidy)

⚘ Some words sound alike but are spelt differently and have different meanings. Some of these words are in the box below.

⚘ From the box, write the correct word for each picture.

```
road rode;        maid made;        mail male
      clothes close;            wood would
```

_____

_____

_____   _____   _____

90

✱ Words which sound alike but are spelt differently and have different meanings are called homophones. Match the meanings to the homophones.

1. sixty minutes

2. arranged objects in lines

3. belonging to us

4. the opposite of yes

5. water droplets from the sky

6. a flower

7. to learn or understand something

8. belonging to them

9. to rule as a king or queen

10. a place

our
hour

rows
rose

no
know

rain
reign

there
their

❀ **Choose the correct homophones to complete the sentences.**

rows, rose

1. I gave mummy a red ___________.
2. The chairs were placed in four ___________.

there, their

3. Are ___________ any fruits left?
4. They ate all of ___________ lunch.

our, hour

5. ___________ church is having a harvest.
6. It starts in an ___________.

know, no

7. Do you ___________ the answer to the question?
8. ___________, I do not.

✤ **Choose the correct homophone for each space.**

1. I can _____ some boats on the _____.
   (sea, see)

2. Anna _____ all _____ plums. (ate, eight)

3. _____ will you _____ that dress?
   (wear, where)

4. _____ of our boys _____ first prize.
   (one, won)

5. The _____ shirt _____ off the line.
   (blew, blue)

6. Did you _____ your name on the _____
   side of the paper? (write, right)

7. Tyler _____ his bicycle down the _____.
   (road, rode)

8. Did you read the _____ about a dog without a
   _____. (tail, tale)

✿ **Match the meanings to the homophones.**

1. seven days

2. a mixture of flour and water

3. not strong

4. when the body hurts

5. a portion or part of a whole

6. glass in a window or door

7. a large sea animal

8. a female rabbit or deer

9. the total

10. a cry of pain

weak

week

pain

pane

dough

doe

some

sum

wail

whale

✿ **Finish the words to complete the sentences.**

1. There are seven days in one **we**_____.

2. He fell and had a **pa**_____ in his leg.

3. What is the **s**_____ of three plus twelve?

4. A **w**_____ is not a fish.

5. Please may I have **s**_____ lunch?

6. The boy gave a loud **w**_____ when he fell.

7. Grandma kneaded the **do**_____ for the salt bread.

8. I was sick and I felt very **we**_____.

9. The ball broke the window **pa**_____.

10. Put the **do**_____ and the buck in that hutch.

✦ **Compound words are formed when we join two words. Match these words to form compound words. Write the words formed on the lines.**

space   cycle

_____

sail   plane

_____

air   ship

_____

motor   lift

_____

wheel   boat

_____

fork   chair

_____

✿ Choose words from the box to form compound words for the pictures below.

super	works	bed	**fall**	sun	house
water	flower	light	market	room	fire

Example:

waterfall

_____

_____

_____

_____

_____

✿ Use these words to make compound words with the word 'book'.   Example: workbook

shelf	cook
text	worm
case	hymn

_____

_____

_____

_____

_____

❀ **Complete the alphabet.**

a	b			e	f		h	i			l	m		o		q	r		t	u			w			z

❀ **Arrange these letters in alphabetical order.**

Example:

1. c   d   a   b

   <u> **a**   **b**   **c**   **d** </u>

2. h   f   g   i

   <u>   </u>

3. w   z   x   v   y

   <u>   </u>

4. k   o   r   y   s

   <u>   </u>

5. o   e   u   a   i

   <u>   </u>

6. v   m   b   h   t

   <u>   </u>

❀ **Arrange these letters in alphabetical order.**

Example:

Example		1		2		3		4	
k	**e**	l		o		h		f	
i	**g**	g		m		d		n	
m	**i**	q		d		s		k	
g	**k**	w		r		r		p	
e	**m**	s		f		e		o	

98

✻ Arrange the words below in alphabetical order. The first letter in each word is different. Look at the first letter only.

Example:

den
ant
ball
cart

ant
ball
cart
den

1
cherry
apple
dunks
banana

2
goat
fish
egret
horse

This one is done for you.

3.   jump,   skip,   hop,   fly

___**fly,   hop,   jump,   skip**___

4.   six,   four,   eight,   two

_____

5.   car,   van,   bus,   truck

_____

6.   Monday,   Tuesday,   Wednesday,   Friday

_____

✿ Arrange the words below in alphabetical order. The first letter in each word is the same so look at the second letter.

Example:

toes		tag
tip		tent
tag		tip
turn		toes
tent		turn

1	pit		
	pat		
	pot		
	put		
	pet		

2	shop		
	slip		
	scar		
	step		
	swing		

3.   cycle,   check,   coat,   cricket,   clap

_____

4.   twin,   tyre,   thick,   track,   tube

_____

5.   slap,   star,   scar,   smart,   shake

_____

✿ Write the alphabet in the boxes.

✿ Arrange these words in alphabetical order.

1 | yellow | |
red	
orange	
green	
purple	

2 | spoon | |
fork	
knife	
plate	
cup	

3 | snore | |
scar	
smart	
sport	
skip	

4 | burn | |
blue	
brown	
bark	
bike	

5 | pigeon | |
turkey	
swan	
duck	
goose	

6 | taste | |
smell	
hear	
feel	
see	

✿ Write the alphabet in the boxes. Then arrange the words below in alphabetical order.

.1.   run, jump, skip, hop, flip

_____

2.   chain, centre, clock, cube, crush

_____

3.   jeep, truck, plane, van, boat

_____

4.   okra, tomato, cucumber, pumpkin, squash

_____

5.   yo-yo, frisbee, doll, blocks, puzzle

_____

6.   peas, pram, phone, point, plant

_____

7.   strap, snake, ship, sort, skip

_____

8.   triangle, rectangle, circle, square, pentagon

_____

✿ Words which have the same meaning are called synonyms. In each box, circle the synonym for the first word.

happy	*sick*	*equal*
glad	sorry	unequal
sad	well	same
angry	ill	quarter

large	*neat*	*quiet*
long	near	still
charge	tidy	loud
huge	never	quick

wrong	*part*	*begin*
right	start	commence
incorrect	whole	end
wrote	fraction	before

❋ **Rewrite each sentence replacing the underlined word with a synonym from the box.**

end, beat, show, hard, answer, wealthy, middle, harm

1 Rhianna is very *rich*.

_____

2. The police did not *hurt* the man.

_____

3. Were the cars on *display* ?

_____

4. The movie came to a sudden *finish*.

_____

5. Most people say that Mathematics is *difficult*.

_____

6. Do you think we can *defeat* Hilda Skeene ?

_____

7. You should always *reply* politely.

_____

8. Her car broke down in the *centre* of the road.

_____

Section 7

- Telling sentences
- Asking sentences
- Question Words
- Helping Words
- Punctuation marks

Joining sentences with

- But
- And

✿ A telling sentence is a sentence which gives information or makes a statement. It begins with a capital letter and ends with a full stop. Write these telling sentences correctly.

Example: coconut water is a refreshing drink

Coconut water is a refreshing drink.

1. the hurricane season starts on June 1st

_____

2. i have to go horseback riding on Saturday

_____

3. children were buying tamarind balls

_____

✿ Write a telling sentence using the word given in the brackets.

Example: (cat) A cat has whiskers.

1. (bicycle)

_____

2. (mother)

_____

3. (dog)

_____

❀ An asking sentence or question is a sentence which asks for information. It begins with a capital letter and ends with a question mark. Write these questions correctly.

Example: have you ever been to Oistins Fish Fry

Have you ever been to Oistins Fish Fry**?**

1. what is the national flower of Barbados

_____

2. where is Culpepper Island

_____

3. do you go swimming at the Aquatic Centre

_____

❀ Write a question using the word given in the brackets.

Example: (did) Did you do your homework?

1. (what)

_____

2. (how)

_____

3. (why)

_____

✿ Question words are found at the beginning of sentences to help ask questions. Choose the correct question word from the brackets to complete each sentence.

1. _____ is your sister? (why, when, where)

2. _____ sports do you like? (how, what, when)

3. _____ book is this? (whose, when, where)

4. _____ many snacks did you buy?
(why, how, whose)

5. _____ would you like to meet me?
(which, when, what)

✿ Circle the question words in each box.

1.
```
where,   they,   which,   like,   this,   why
```

2.
```
those,   who,   look,   here,   what,   help
```

3.
```
how,   that,   now,   there,   whose,   when
```

✿ Verbs which are placed at the beginning of sentences to help ask questions are called helping verbs. Choose the correct verb from the brackets to complete each question.

1. _____ you like watching movies? (were, was, do)

2. _____ you seen my ball? (shall, have, does)

3. _____ they cooking soup? (are, can, had)

4. _____ she an athlete? (has, is, may)

5. _____ you be my friend? (am, was, will)

✿ **Circle the verbs in each box <u>which help ask questions</u>.**

.1. | about, have, hate, has, with, had |

2. | am, take, are, is, there, held |

3. | cope, do, now, that, does, did |

4. | may, that, thank, will, alike, shall |

✽ **Commas are used to separate items or things in a list. Put commas in the sentences to separate the items.**

Example: I found shells rocks and crabs on the sand.

I found shells, rocks and crabs on the sand.

1. Pamela bought turnovers sweetbread and pone.

2. Tables chairs beds and benches are furniture.

3. Did you see the toolkit with the hammer saw drill and screwdriver?

4. Bico sells vanilla chocolate and coconut ice cream.

5. We had drinks popcorn hotdogs sweets and cake.

6. He bought books pencils sharpeners rubbers and rulers.

7. Did you pack the plates knives forks napkins and cups?

8. Nicoli plays football cricket tennis rugby and volleyball.

9. Apples mangoes oranges grapes and dunks are fruits.

10. Lukas used yellow green orange red and blue paints.

✲ **The apostrophe is used to show possession. Write an apostrophe to show who owns each thing.**

Example: The kite belonging to Trozary. <u>Trozary's kite</u>

1. The chair belonging to Grandma. _____.

2. The truck belonging to Mike. _____.

3. The friend of Jan. _____.

4. The boat belonging to the men. _____.

5. The tails belonging to the mice. _____.

✾ **Write the phrases correctly with apostrophes.**

Example: the mans bicycle

the man's bicycle

this boys bat

the gooses feathers

one cats whiskers

this sheeps pen

the books leaf

the womans handbag

this tables leg

a childs pram

✾ **Put an apostrophe correctly in each sentence.**

1. Red Hens friends did not help her.

2. Rapunzels hair was very long.

3. Cinderellas stepsisters disliked her.

4. Jacks mother was angry with him.

5. Goldilocks ate Baby Bears porridge.

✿ Write the phrases below correctly with apostrophes. The apostrophe is placed on the outside of plural nouns which end with 's'.

Example: two girls dolls

                two girls' dolls

four flags poles

the boxes labels

three dogs collars

some fishes scales

several players bats

the ladies scarves

these chefs hats

the knives blades

✿ Put an apostrophe correctly in each sentence.

1. Five houses roofs were blown off.

2. Those books leaves were torn out.

3. The churches doors are always open.

4. The two boats sails had holes.

❀ Apostrophes can also be used to show that letters have been omitted from words or to shorten them.

Examples:

I am	it is	you are	they have
I'm	it's	you're	they've

❀ Shorten the words below by omitting the circled letters.

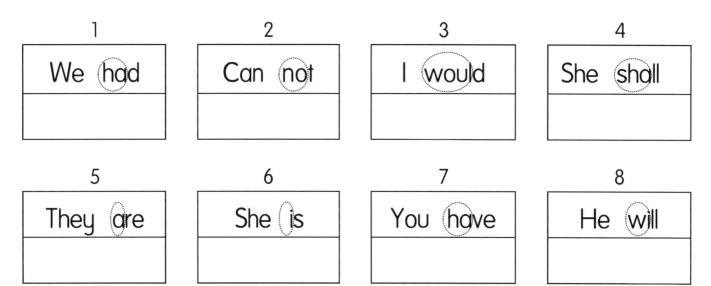

1	2	3	4
We had	Can not	I would	She shall

5	6	7	8
They are	She is	You have	He will

❀ Put an apostrophe correctly in each sentence.

1. Were not going to the party.

2. Shell pay for the tickets.

3. Ive not seen that movie.

4. Chad cant run very fast.

114

✿ Put an apostrophe correctly in each sentence.

1. Her mothers car is blue.

2. My sisters name is Carol.

3. I cant lift the box.

4. We are going to Pauls birthday party.

5. Im not feeling well.

6. Well take the bus.

7. My fathers sister is my aunt.

8. Our schools PTA meets on Saturdays.

9. Youve done your best.

10. Theyll go to the church picnic.

✿ The exclamation mark is used to express strong feelings like anger, excitement, fear or surprise. Write exclamation marks at the end of the words in the boxes.

Examples:

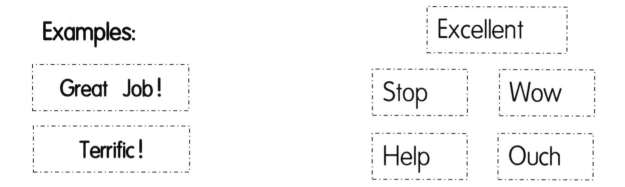

Great Job!

Terrific!

Excellent

Stop   Wow

Help   Ouch

✿ Complete the sentences with exclamation marks.

Examples:

Ouch I stubbed my toe.
Ouch! I stubbed my toe.

Freeze Do not move
Freeze! Do not move!

1. Watch out

2. Wow! That is so amazing

3. Hooray We are going on holiday!

4. Stop it That is not nice.

5. Yippee I have won bingo

116

❀ **Put in the punctuation mark or marks needed for each sentence.**

1. We saw lions tigers and zebras at the zoo.

2. We must keep our classroom clean

3. Do you think it will rain today

4. Stop hitting me

5. There is heavy traffic on the roads

6. Joes brother is twelve years old.

7. Hurry We will miss the bus.

8. The boys foot is broken

9. We saw peacocks egrets swans and pelicans

10. Didnt they win the football match

�֍ **We usually use but to join sentences with different ideas. Use 'but' to join these sentences.**

Example: He is happy. She is sad.

He is happy **but s**he is sad.

1. A fish can swim. It cannot walk.

_____

2. Her room is tidy. His room is untidy.

_____

3. The box is big. It is not heavy.

_____

4. The radio is on. I cannot hear it.

_____

5. We planted many seeds. They did not grow.

_____

6. They have marbles. They cannot pitch.

_____

7. Jerry fell. He did not cry.

_____

✿ **We usually use 'and' to join sentences with similar ideas or to give more information. Use 'and' to join these sentences.**

Example: I can draw. I can colour.

I can draw **and** colour.

1. He has a pencil. He has a rubber.

_____

2. They like playing football. They like playing cricket.

_____

3. Heidi is baking chicken. Heidi is baking potatoes.

_____

4. They took a ferry. They went to St. Vincent.

_____

5. Damien painted a picture. Damien sold it.

_____

6. We pulled out weeds. We planted okra seeds.

_____

7. Boys like lollipops. Girls like lollipops.

_____

Section 8

Verbs

- Identifying verbs

- Continuous tense

- Present tense

- Do, does

- Go, goes

- Past tense

- Opposites

✿ Verbs are action words. Write the verb from the box for each picture.

sail   fly   rain   swing   water

drink   weed   spray   plant

_____

_____

_____

_____

_____

_____

_____

_____

_____

✿ **Choose a suitable verb from the box to complete each sentence.**

```
crawls      swim      chirps      arrive

barks       race      shine       open
```

1. A dog _____ at the cars.

2. Ten cars _____ on the track.

3. Some fishes _____ in the aquarium.

4. The bird _____ in the cage.

5. The stars _____ brightly.

6. A few stores _____ at 8 o'clock.

7. Did the buses _____ late?

8. The baby _____ on the floor.

✿ **Write 'V' above the verbs in the story and then write the verbs in the box below.**

> V
> Some boys play cricket on the pasture. Ben
> runs in and bowls the ball quickly. John swings
> and hits the ball in the air. Ron dives to his
> left and catches the ball with one hand. Dan,
> the umpire, raises his hand and signals 'out'.
> The boys enjoy the game very much.

play _____   _____

_____   _____

_____   _____

_____   _____

✿ We add 'ing' to verbs to form the continuous tense. It shows ongoing action. Complete the table with the continuous tense of the verbs. The first one is done for you.

Verb	Continuous Tense
jump	jumping
play	
sing	
draw	

Verb	Continuous Tense
fry	
wash	
eat	
watch	

✿ Form the continuous tense of the verbs in the brackets and complete the sentences.

Example: The baby is _____sleeping_____ in the cot. (sleep)

1. Mother is _____ breadfruit cou-cou. (cook)

2. We were _____ for her to get well. (pray)

3. Is he _____ the Advocate newspaper? (read)

4. I was not _____ well. (see)

5. Why is the boy _____? (cry)

❀ Some verbs which end with 'e' form their continuous tense by:

(1) taking off the 'e'   (2) adding 'ing'

Example: give   →   giv   →   giv**ing**

❀ Complete the table with the continuous tense of the verbs.

Verb		Continuous Tense
	Take off the 'e'	Add 'ing'
come	com	com**ing**
dine		
save		
use		
hope		
chase		
smoke		

✾ **Complete the sentences with the continuous tense of the verbs in the brackets.**

1. The bartender is _____ coconut punch. (serve)

2. You are _____ me wrongfully. (blame)

3. Is he _____ in St. James? (live)

4. We were _____ many calls. (receive)

5. Is she _____ well today? (behave)

6. The boys were _____ the dogs. (bathe)

7. Is he _____ to New York? (move)

8. Were they line _____ at the party? (dance)

9. We were _____ the pictures in our books. (glue)

10. Mother was _____ the potatoes to make steamed pudding. (grate)

✤ Some verbs which have a vowel just before the consonant at the end, form their continuous tense by:

(1) doubling the last letter   (2) adding 'ing'

Example: put →   putt   →   putting

✤ Complete the table with the continuous tense of the verbs.

Verb	Double the last letter	Continuous Tense Add 'ing'
bat	batt	batting
clap		
pin		
travel		
knit		
refer		
shut		

❀ **Complete the sentences with the continuous tense of the verbs in the brackets.**

1. The butcher is _____ up the meat. (chop)

2. The bride and groom are _____ the cake. (cut)

3. We were slowly _____ our drinks. (sip)

4. She is _____ her job for another one. (quit)

5. The nurse is _____ the patient's leg. (wrap)

6. Are they _____ a trench to lay pipes? (dig)

7. We were _____ the Christmas tree today. (trim)

8. Chris Gayle was _____ many sixes. (hit)

9. Dale is _____ an exam next week. (sit)

10. The teachers are _____ our test. (set)

✿ **Complete the sentences with the continuous tense of the verbs in the brackets.**

1. Someone is _____ at the door. (knock)

2. Are they _____ money for a trip? (save)

3. When are you _____ your party? (plan)

4. The cadet is _____ his boots. (clean)

5. Is he _____ for groceries? (shop)

6. The soldiers are _____ on the Savannah. (march)

7. We are _____ pictures in our books. (paste)

8. The women are _____ cotton. (pick)

9. The gardener is _____ the hedge. (trim)

10. The secretary is _____ a letter. (type)

✿ When speaking in the present tense about singular words we add 's' to most verbs.

Examples:

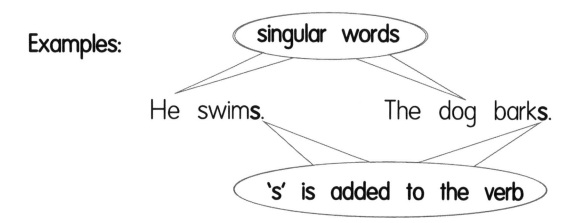

✿ Complete the table below by adding 's' to the verbs.

Verb	Present Tense
visit	He **visit**s
fall	The rain
walk	It
shout	The girl

Verb	Present Tense
pray	Lana
leap	The athlete
bounce	A ball
light	This torch

✿ Complete each sentence with the present tense of the verb in the brackets.

1. Arion _____ a beautiful picture. (draw)

2. The chef _____ the fruits for the salad. (slice)

3. A balloon _____ by in the air. (float)

4. The truck _____ on the highway. (speed)

✿ When speaking in the present tense about singular words, we add 'es' to the verbs which end with 'ch', 'sh', 's', 'ss', 'x', or 'z'.

Examples:

singular words

She catch**es**.   Mummy wash**es**.

'es' is added to the verbs

✿ Complete the table below by adding 'es' to the verbs.

Verb	Present Tense
wish	She **wish**es
teach	My aunt
cross	He
crash	The car

Verb	Present Tense
fizz	His drink
fish	Uncle
bless	The priest
fix	A plumber

✿ Complete each sentence with the present tense of the verb in the brackets.

1. The dog runs and _____ the ball. (fetch)

2. The dancer _____ across the floor. (waltz)

3. Daddy _____ in the patio. (relax)

4. The maid _____ clothes daily. (wash)

✿ When speaking in the present tense about plural words and the words 'you' and 'I' we <u>do not</u> add 's' or 'es' to the verb.

Examples:

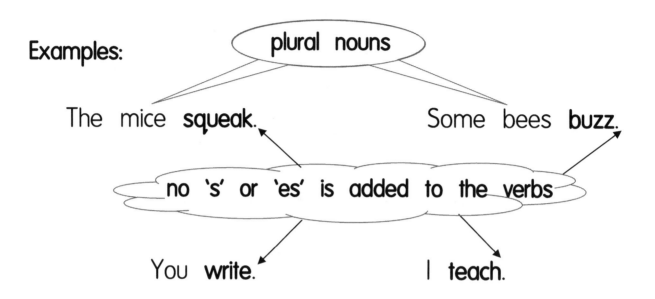

plural nouns

The mice **squeak**.   Some bees **buzz**.

no 's' or 'es' is added to the verbs

You **write**.   I **teach**.

✿ Write an appropriate word in the space to complete each sentence.

Example: Her ____cats____ like to eat fish.

1. His _____ bark as the people pass by.

2. My _____ sleep all day long.

3. _____ gallop around the track.

4. The _____ stitch the uniforms.

5. The _____ play checkers.

132

✿ **Underline the correct word in the brackets to complete each sentence.**

1. Jonathan (give, gives) a flower to his teacher.

2. Mongooses (like, likes) to eat chickens.

3. The children (blow, blows) bubbles at the party.

4. My feet (hurt, hurts).

5. Jockey Patrick Husbands (win, wins) many races.

6. He (teach, teaches) windsurfing.

7. You and I (dive, dives) into the pool quickly.

8. The tourists (relax, relaxes) on the beach.

9. My father (prefer, prefers) cricket to football.

10. The vendors (sell, sells) clothes at the flea market.

✽ These verbs all end with 'y'. Circle the verb if a vowel comes before the last letter.

| cry | stay | marry | hurry | enjoy | empty |
| pray | study | play | carry | obey | destroy |

✽ Now sort the verbs in the correct boxes.

Vowel
just before the 'y'

employ

_____

_____

_____

_____

_____

Consonant
just before the 'y'

try

_____

_____

_____

_____

_____

134

* **Verbs which end with 'y' and have a vowel just before the 'y', add 's' when used with singular words in the present tense.**

* **Complete the sentences by writing the present tense of each verb in the brackets.**

Example: Aunty ___buys___ a tablet for me. (buy)

1. The hen _____ eggs in the nest. (lay)

2. The netball team _____ matches at the stadium. (play)

3. The loud barking _____ mother. (annoy)

4. Daddy _____ the credit card bill online. (pay)

5. She _____ away from school too often. (stay)

6. A storm _____ crops. (destroy)

7. Any child who _____, is punished. (disobey)

8. The principal _____ that she is pleased with our behaviour. (say)

✿ Verbs which end with 'y' and have a consonant just before the 'y', change the 'y' to 'i' and add 'es' when used with singular words in the present tense.

Example: carry   →   carri   →   carri**es**

✿ Complete the table with the present tense of the verbs.

Verb	Change 'y' to 'i'	Present Tense
		Add 'es'
cry	cri	cri**es**
hurry		
empty		
marry		
fry		

✿ Write the present tense of the verb in each space.

1. The boy _____ hard at his school work. (try)

2. She _____ her homework quickly. (copy)

3. Daren often _____ his bedroom. (tidy)

4. Mother _____ about the children. (worry)

136

❀ We use the verb 'goes' when we speak about singular words and 'go' when we speak about plural words. We always use 'go' with the words 'you' and 'I'.

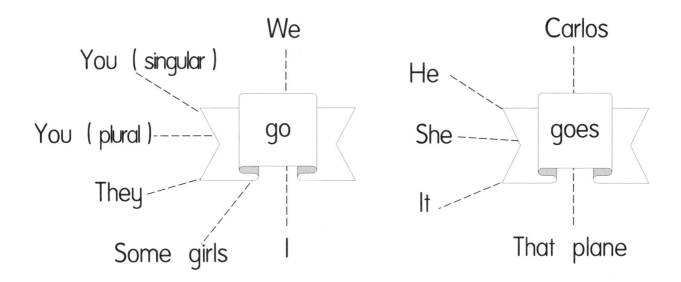

❀ **Underline 'go' or 'goes' to complete the sentences.**

1. He (go, goes) to lessons on Saturdays.

2. Do you (go, goes) to Miami Beach?

3. I (go, goes) to bed at eight o'clock.

4. It (go, goes) around very quickly.

5. Mark and I (go, goes) fishing on weekends.

✤ **We use the verb 'does' when we speak about singular words and 'do' when we speak about plural words. We always use 'do' with the words 'you' and 'I'.**

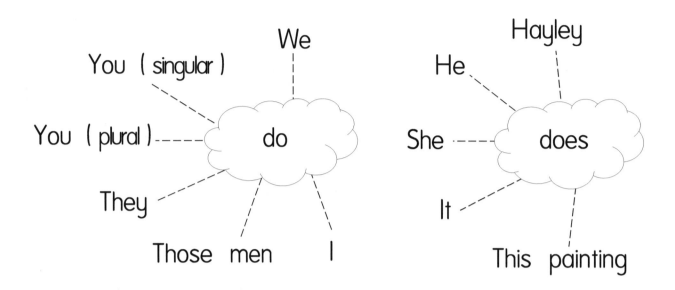

✤ **Underline 'do' or 'does' to complete the sentences.**

1. She (do, does) not hear very well.

2. (Do, Does) we need to buy cassava?

3. It (do, does) look very pretty.

4. (Do, Does) you want to come with me?

5. I (do, does) not like to sleep in the dark.

✿ Complete the tables correctly with 'go' and 'goes'.

Every mini van	
Another doctor	

This pony	
Several buses	

You	
A few buses	

Rick and Joe	
It	

Neither girl	
Three children	

Either bus	
She	

✿ Complete the tables correctly with 'do' and 'does'.

That book	
Most bays	

Some churches	
The boy	

We	
A cook	

They	
That potato	

The nurse	
It	

He and I	
I	

❀ **Complete the tables with the past tense of the verbs.**

Present Tense	Past Tense
eat	ate
dig	
fall	
get	
win	
am	
tell	
feed	
sink	
tear	
ring	
meet	
wear	
speak	

Present Tense	Past Tense
see	
have	
give	
take	
ride	
are	
hide	
drive	
wake	
rise	
shake	
leave	
shine	
become	

✿ **Complete the lines of the nursery rhymes with the past tense of the words in the brackets.**

1. Humpty Dumpty _____ on the wall. (sit)

2. Jack and Jill _____ up the hill to fetch a pail of water. (go)

3. Mary _____ a little lamb. (has)

4. Old King Cole _____ a merry old soul. (is)

5. Once, I _____ a fish alive. (catch)

6. Georgie Porgie kissed the girls and _____ them cry. (make)

7. Tom, Tom the Piper's son _____ a pig and away he _____. (steal) (run)

8. Jack _____ down and broke his crown and Jill _____ tumbling after. (fall) (come)

✿ **Form the past tense of the words in the brackets and complete the sentences.**

1. The show _____ at 5 o'clock. (begin)

2. Mummy _____ my bedroom. (sweep)

3. I _____ the loud cry of the baby. (hear)

4. The plants _____ very tall. (grow)

5. He _____ me for many years. (know)

6. She _____ me how to tie my laces. (teach)

7. Last night, I _____ soundly. (sleep)

8. I _____ out the candles on my cake. (blow)

9. He _____ on tightly to the kite string. (hold)

10. Many children _____ to do their homework. (forget)

✾ We add 'ed' to most verbs to show past tense or action that is finished.

Example: Today I climb. (**present tense**)

Yesterday I climb**ed**. (**past tense**)

✾ Form the past tense of these verbs.

Present Tense	Past Tense
work	work**ed**
1. chew	_____
2. water	_____
3. paint	_____
4. talk	_____
5. pitch	_____
6. cook	_____
7. pull	_____
8. watch	_____
9. fix	_____
10. add	_____

✽ **Form the past tense of the words in the brackets and complete the sentences.**

1. The dog _____ at the cat. (bark)

2. Last year, I _____ my aunt in Antigua. (visit)

3. I _____ a box of cereal this morning. (open)

4. That car _____ into the pole. (crash)

5. He _____ at home because he was sick. (stay)

6. I _____ my sums carefully. (check)

7. The snow cone _____ quickly. (melt)

8. The coach _____ at the players. (shout)

9. We _____ home yesterday. (walk)

10. The West Indies _____ six more runs to win the match. (need)

✿ Most verbs which end with 'e' form their past tense by adding 'd'.

Example: Today we race. (**present tense**)

Yesterday we race**d**. (**past tense**)

✿ Form the past tense of these verbs.

Present Tense	Past Tense
live	live**d**
1. paste	
2. joke	
3. dice	
4. care	
5. blame	
6. tie	
7. hope	
8. dive	
9. surprise	
10. believe	

✱ **Form the past tense of the verbs in the brackets and complete the sentences.**

1. Daddy _____ the leaves. (rake)

2. I _____ my hand to answer the question. (raise)

3. Mummy _____ macaroni pie and sweetbread for the picnic. (bake)

4. When she _____ at me, I felt happy. (smile)

5. Uncle _____ the coconut with the new grater. (grate)

6. We _____ to the calypso beat. (dance)

7. The dog _____ the cat around the garden. (chase)

8. Dave and I _____ the movie. (hate)

9. The children _____ well in the church. (behave)

10. They _____ the chocolate cake. (like)

✿ Make the verbs past tense and write them in the correct boxes.

| doze | jump | ache | see | ride | fetch |
| push | breathe | forget | give | help | glare |

Add 'ed'				

Add 'd'				

Change the Word				

✿ Complete the sentences with the past tense of the verbs in the brackets.

1. They _____ the bus to Bank Hall. (catch)

2. Mary _____ the plane ride. (hate)

3. We _____ attentively to the teacher. (listen)

4. The concert _____ at 6 o'clock. (begin)

5. He _____ money at the credit union. (save)

✿ Most verbs which have one syllable and have a vowel just before the consonant at the end, form their past tense by:

(1) doubling the last letter   (2) adding 'ed'

Example: bat →   batt   →   batt**ed**

✿ Complete the table with the past tense of the verbs.

Present Tense		Past Tense
Verb	Double the last letter	Add 'ed'
stop	stop**p**	stop**ped**
hem		
jog		
knit		
hum		
tap		
whip		

✤ **Form the past tense of the words in the brackets and complete the sentences.**

1. We _____ our drinks. (sip)

2. They _____ each other and said goodbye. (hug)

3. The janitor _____ the classroom. (mop)

4. Aunty _____ a sweater for me. (knit)

5. The children _____ with a long rope. (skip)

6. The teacher _____ when I asked to go to the bathroom. (nod)

7. They were _____ in the cave for days. (trap)

8. The hungry woman _____ for food. (beg)

9. Frank _____ on a banana peel. (slip)

10. The head girl _____ the corsage on the Governor General's jacket. (pin)

⚘ **Verbs which end with 'y' and have a vowel just before the 'y' form their past tense by adding 'ed'.**

⚘ **Form the past tense of the words in the brackets and complete the sentences.**

1. Hurricane Janet _____ many homes. (destroy)

2. The cricket team _____ a match at Pickwick. (play)

3. Joel _____ Sara by blowing the whistle in her ear. (annoy)

4. The farmer _____ the crops for pest. (spray)

5. The bus was _____ for half an hour. (delay)

6. Suki King _____ playing draughts. (enjoy)

7. My sisters _____ for Paul to get well. (pray)

8. John and James _____ their parents. (obey)

9. We _____ at home because of the strike. (stay)

10. The trees _____ in the strong winds. (sway)

❀ Verbs which end with 'y' and have a consonant just before the 'y' form their past tense by:

(1) changing the 'y' to 'i'   (2) adding 'ed'

Example: hurry   →   hurri   →   hurried

❀ Complete the table with the past tense of the verbs.

Present Tense		Past Tense
Verb	Change 'y' to 'i'	Add 'ed'
fry	fri	fried
tidy		
cry		
copy		
apply		
worry		
empty		

✿ **Form the past tense of the verbs in the brackets and complete the sentences.**

1. The dog _____ the bone in the dirt. (bury)

2. Grandma _____ the sorrel in the sun. (dry)

3. They got _____ at St. Patrick's Church. (marry)

4. We _____ our best but still lost the match. (try)

5. The children _____ the homework from the chalkboard. (copy)

6. We _____ our trays to the lunchroom. (carry)

7. The vendor _____ the fish cakes in a buck pot. (fry)

8. She _____ to catch the bus. (hurry)

9. Were the bins _____ yesterday? (empty)

10. Daddy _____ when we were out late. (worry)

✿ In the table below are some irregular verbs that end with 'y'. Choose the correct past tense from the box and complete the table.

> said,   bought,   flew,   paid,   laid

Present Tense	pay	fly	lay	buy	say
Past Tense					

✿ Complete the sentences with the past tenses from above.

1. The birds _____ over the building.

2. We _____ snacks from the canteen.

3. He _____ that he was sorry.

4. Mummy _____ the water bill.

5. The hen _____ two eggs.

✤ **Make the verbs past tense and write them in the correct boxes.**

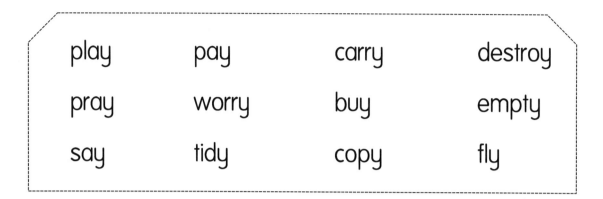

play	pay	carry	destroy
pray	worry	buy	empty
say	tidy	copy	fly

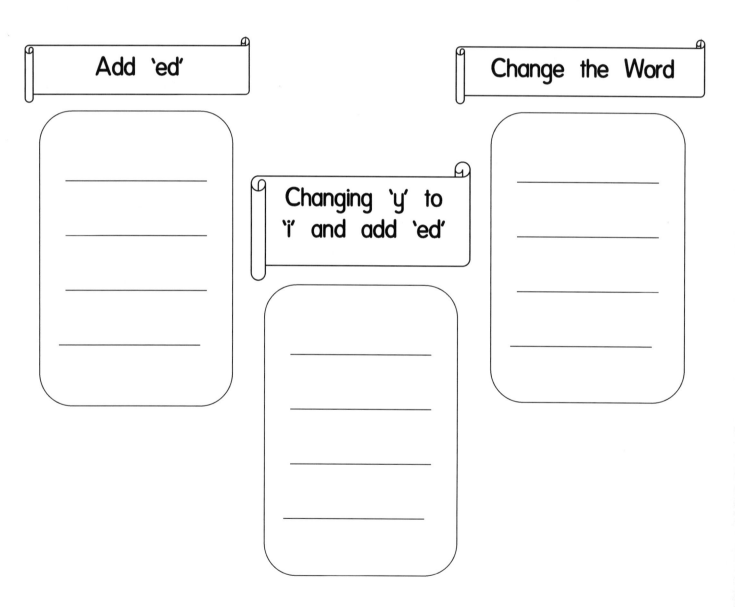

Add 'ed'

_____

_____

_____

_____

Changing 'y' to 'i' and add 'ed'

_____

_____

_____

_____

Change the Word

_____

_____

_____

✿ **Copy the story and change the verbs from the present tense to past tense.**

Some tourists **plan** a trip to Barbados. They **pay** for their tickets online. The plane **flies** from New York to Barbados. They **arrive** in the afternoon. They each **carry** one suitcase. After one week, they **leave** the island. They **say** they **enjoy** their stay in Barbados.

Section 9

Adjectives

- Quantity, size & colour
- Appealing to the senses
- Conditions & emotions
- Ending with 'y'

❀ Adjectives are words which describe nouns. Shade the circle next to the word which best describes each picture. The first one is done for you.

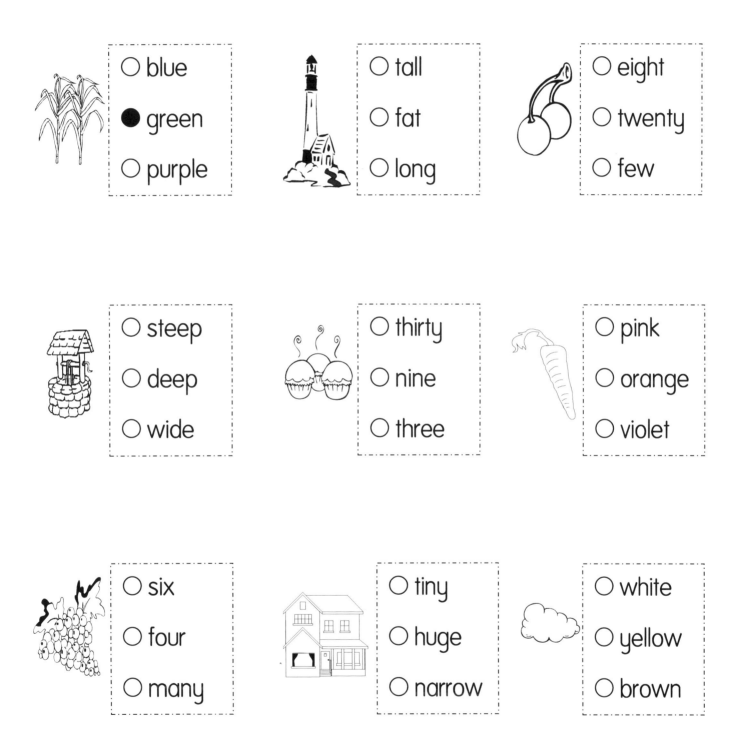

○ blue
● green
○ purple

○ tall
○ fat
○ long

○ eight
○ twenty
○ few

○ steep
○ deep
○ wide

○ thirty
○ nine
○ three

○ pink
○ orange
○ violet

○ six
○ four
○ many

○ tiny
○ huge
○ narrow

○ white
○ yellow
○ brown

❀ **Adjectives can describe the colour, size, number or quantity of nouns. Sort these adjectives in the correct columns.**

small	grey	some	broad	purple	twenty
dozen	black	gold	slender	deep	single

Number / Quantity	Size	Colour

❀ **Circle the two adjectives in each sentence.**

1. There are five purple flowers in the pot.
2. She has big, brown eyes.
3. Do you have seven pink bows?
4. I had a long, white tail on my kite.
5. Many small seeds are in the tray.

⊛ **Circle the adjectives in each sentence.**

1. May I have two yellow lollipops?

2. He bought some large containers.

3. Put sixteen white chairs in each row.

4. Are there many red cars in the race?

5. My dog has four chubby brown puppies.

⊛ **Complete the sentences with suitable adjectives. Use the words in the brackets to help you.**

1. He has a _____ _____ marble.
                      (size   colour)

2. _____ _____ mangoes are in the tree.
    (number   colour)

3. There are _____ _____ bottles standing
   on the wall. (number   colour)

4. The road is _____ and _____.
                  (size   size)

✿ We use our senses to tell how nouns look, feel, sound, taste or smell. Sort the adjectives below in the most suitable box.

smooth   noisy   smoky   untidy   pretty

sticky   delicious   loud   burnt   hard

quiet   musty   handsome   sour   bitter

sound _____ _____ _____

feel _____ _____ _____

taste _____ _____ _____

look _____ _____ _____

smell _____ _____ _____

✿ **Circle each adjective and underline the noun it describes.**

Example: We ate (juicy) <u>mangoes</u>.

1. We drove on the bumpy road.

2. A cool breeze blows through the window.

3. She speaks in a squeaky voice.

4. There are rotten soursops under the tree.

5. Loud music blared from the speakers.

6. The moon is round.

7. The conkie was delicious.

8. This roti is too spicy.

9. The drinks are very cold.

10. The room was very quiet when we entered.

✽ **Write a suitable adjective in the space to complete the sentences. Each adjective must be different.**

1. I have a _____ ball.

2. These benches are very _____.

3. The music is too _____.

4. There are many _____ flowers in the garden.

5. Was the food _____?

6. This perfume smells _____.

7. Sam always keeps a _____ room.

8. The water from the sea taste _____.

9. Barbados has _____ parishes.

10. Did you buy a _____ ice cream?

✤ Shade the circle next to the adjective which best describes each picture.

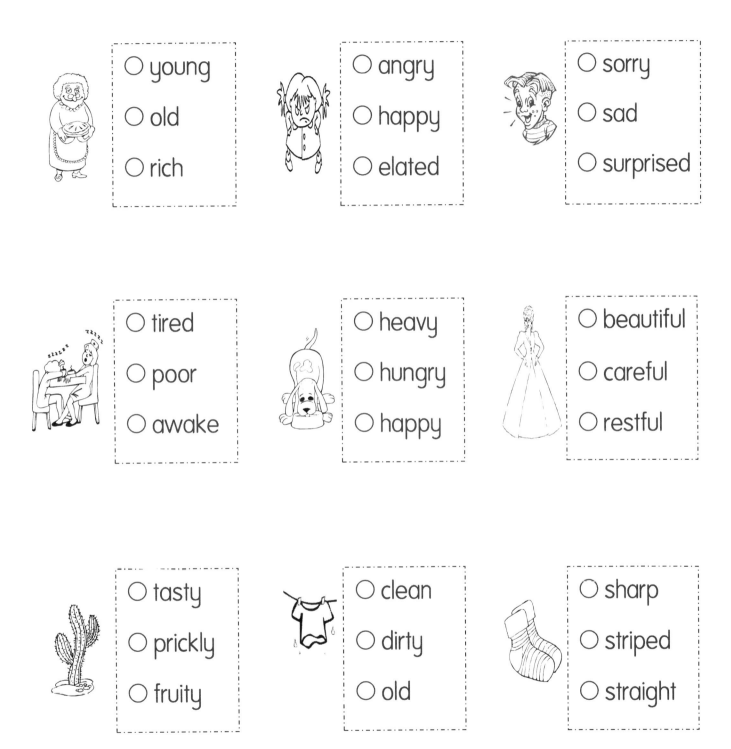

○ young
○ old
○ rich

○ angry
○ happy
○ elated

○ sorry
○ sad
○ surprised

○ tired
○ poor
○ awake

○ heavy
○ hungry
○ happy

○ beautiful
○ careful
○ restful

○ tasty
○ prickly
○ fruity

○ clean
○ dirty
○ old

○ sharp
○ striped
○ straight

✽ **We use adjectives to describe how people are feeling. Choose the most suitable adjective to complete each sentence.**

> elated,   annoyed,   scared,   jealous,   unhappy

1. John felt _____ when the dog chased him.

2. Hendy is _____ because he lost his pet.

3. Joseph's brothers were _____ when his father gave him a coat.

4. David was _____ because he was getting a new bicycle.

5. Kyle was _____ when his sister broke his toy.

✽ **Write 'A' above the adjective in each sentence and then write the adjective on the line.**

                         A

Example: The girls are happy. _____happy_____

1. The sad boy is crying. _____

2. The teacher is pleased with my work. _____

3. The angry coach shouts at the players. _____

4. My grandmother is afraid of centipedes. _____

✿ A suffix is added at the end of a word to change its meaning. Adjectives can be formed by adding the suffix 'y' at the end of some nouns.

✿ Form adjectives by adding 'y' to these nouns.

Example:

1. rock ____rocky____

2. lump _____

3. cloud _____

4. crisp _____

5. sand _____

6. thirst _____

7. luck _____

8. mess _____

✿ Complete the sentences using some of the adjectives formed.

1. It is very _____ today.

2. Barbados has white _____ beaches.

3. The porridge was too _ _____.

4. The biscuits were very _____.

5. We were very _____ after playing games.

6. Her room is always _____.

✿ **Choose the most suitable adjective to complete each sentence.**

Example: We heard the _____**loud**_____ ringing of the bell.
    ○ buzz   ○ thump   ● loud

1. He bought a _____ shirt from the store.
    ○ cotton   ○ metal   ○ glass

2. The _____ car over-took the slow one.
    ○ slow   ○ fast   ○ lagging

3. The girl wore a _____ dress to church.
    ○ empty   ○ cold   ○ beautiful

4. The room was _____ and musty.
    ○ sweet   ○ happy   ○ dark

5. We sat on the _____ rock and ate our snacks.
    ○ flat   ○ sticky   ○ soft

6. The teacher was _____ with the naughty child.
    ○ scared   ○ annoyed   ○ surprised

7. The sea was _____ so we took a swim.
    ○ rough   ○ calm   ○ choppy

✹ **Circle the most suitable adjective in the brackets that can replace the one in <u>bold</u>.**

Example: Is he a **tidy** boy? (tall, ⟨neat,⟩ ugly)

1. Jade is a **nice** girl. (pleasant, talkative, naughty)

2. We had a **delicious** meal. (hot, tasty, peppery)

3. The clown performs **wonderful** tricks.
   (many, amazing, high)

4. Acrobats perform **unsafe** stunts.
   (good, many, dangerous)

5. The teacher told us an **interesting** story.
   (exciting, important, horrible)

6. The house was **empty** when we arrived.
   (open, vacant, untidy)

7. The **brave** boy saved the tourist from drowning.
   (short, new, heroic)

8. The **fat** woman walked slowly. (obese, thin, hungry)

⚘ **Write a suitable adjective in each space. Each adjective must be different.**

1. Sara carried a _____ black bag to school.

2. We had lots of fun in the _____ tent.

3. Today, the weather is _____.

4. Did Daddy give mummy twelve _____ roses?

5. The light from the sun is very _____.

6. We watched the _____ cars speed around the track.

7. Donico picked _____ green coconuts.

8. We ate a _____ meal at the luncheon.

9. Adrian felt _____ because he had not eaten all day.

10. In art class, we drew many _____ lines.

✿ Write 'N' for noun, 'V' for verb and 'A' for adjective for the following sentences.

Example:
         N   V   A   N
The boy felt happy after the race.

1. Daddy bought a hammer.

2. The whale swims in the ocean.

3. Grandma takes four pills.

4. The sharp knife cut the butcher.

5. Nurses care for their sick patients.

6. My cousin rides to the supermarket.

7. The cows grazed on the green pasture.

8. Many trees fell during the storm.

9. The hikers walked through a small gully.

10. Some girls wore long skirts to the party.

Homework

	Page / Pages		Page / Pages
1		21	
2		22	
3		23	
4		24	
5		25	
6		26	
7		27	
8		28	
9		29	
10		30	
11		31	
12		32	
13		33	
14		34	
15		35	
16		36	
17		37	
18		38	
19		39	
20		40	

Made in the USA
Columbia, SC
22 August 2024

40364762R00098